LEACH SCHOOL LIBRARY

W9-BGR-451

Doris K. Goodie
210 Woodlawn Ave.
Lot #125
Frankton, IN 46044

Doris K. Goodie
210 Woodlawn Ave.
Lot
Frankton, IN 46044

Doris K. Goodie
210 Woodlawn Ave.
Lot
Frankton,

Doris K. Goodie
210 Woodlawn Ave.
Lot #125
Frankton, IN 46044

Doris K. Goble
210 Woodworth Ave.
Lot #126
Frankton, IN 46044

A Picture Book of

FOREST ANIMALS

Written by Joanne Gise
Illustrated by Roseanna Pistolesi

Doris K. Goble
210 Woodworth Ave.
Frankton, IN 46044

Troll Associates

Library of Congress Cataloging-in-Publication Data
Gise, Joanne.
    A picture book of forest animals / by Joanne Gise; illustrated by
Roseanna Pistolesi.
    p.   cm.
    Summary: Brief text and illustrations introduce twelve forest
animals including the raccoon, brown bear, and skunk.
    ISBN 0-8167-1904-7 (lib. bdg.)   ISBN 0-8167-1905-5 (pbk.)
    1. Forest fauna—Juvenile literature.   [1. Forest animals.]
I. Pistolesi, Roseanna, ill.   II. Title.
QL112.G57 1990
599.0909'52—dc20   89-37329

Copyright © 1990 by Troll Associates, Mahwah, N.J.

All rights reserved. No portion of this book may be reproduced in any
form, electronic or mechanical, including photocopying, recording, or
information storage and retrieval systems, without prior written
permission from the publisher.   Printed in the U S A

10   9   8   7   6   5   4   3   2   1

WHITE-TAILED DEER

Look closely in the long grass. There might be a *fawn*, or baby deer, there. Mother deer hide their babies in the grass. The white spots on a fawn's back make it hard to see.

A fawn's spots disappear as it gets older. Male deer, or *bucks*, grow antlers. These antlers are made of strong bone. They fall off every winter, but every spring they grow back bigger than the year before. Bucks use their antlers when they fight over a *doe*, or female deer. The buck who wins will mate with the doe. In the spring, she will give birth to 1-2 fawns.

RED SQUIRREL

In the fall, you will often see squirrels burying nuts and acorns. When the weather gets cold, squirrels cuddle together in their nests and sleep. When a warm day comes, they wake up—and they are hungry! Then they dig up some of the nuts they buried and have a snack.

Squirrels love to play. They run and jump through
the trees, chase each other, and even hang from
branches by their back feet. Its bushy tail helps the
squirrel keep its balance. Its tail helps the squirrel in
another way. It keeps the squirrel warm when it sleeps!

COTTONTAIL RABBIT

Most animals walk or run. Not the rabbit! It hops. A rabbit's hind legs are much longer than its front legs, and very strong. This lets it hop up to 10 feet. If you come near a rabbit, it will sit very, very still. It is hoping you will walk by without seeing it. But if you come too close—hop! The rabbit jumps away.

Rabbits have lots of babies. Several families, or *litters*, are born every year. There are 2-8 baby rabbits, called *kits*, in each litter. The kits are blind and deaf and have no fur when they are born. But in a few weeks, they are big enough to leave their mother.

RACCOON

The black hair around a raccoon's eyes makes it look like a masked bandit. Raccoons often act like bandits, too. They are very curious. Their front feet are almost like hands, so they can pick up small objects. They can even open garbage can lids—something they do when searching for food. A raccoon will eat just about anything. Berries, frogs, insects, and fish are some of its favorite foods. Raccoons like water and often dip their food in it.

Raccoons like to hunt at night. During the day, they sleep in hollow trees, or even in basements and chimneys! In the winter, raccoons sleep when it is very cold. But on a warm day, they will come outside to eat.

CHIPMUNK

A chipmunk doesn't use its hands to carry things—it uses its cheeks! When a chipmunk finds nuts and seeds, it stores them in pouches in its cheeks. Then it brings them home to eat.

Chipmunks live underground in *burrows*. In the fall, they get ready for winter. They eat and eat until they are round and fat. They also store lots of nuts and seeds in their burrows. A chipmunk sleeps most of the winter. It is snug and warm in its home. It wakes up once in a while to eat some of the seeds it has stored.

OPOSSUM

When opossums are born, they are so small that 20 could fit in a teaspoon! They crawl into a pouch on their mother's stomach and stay there until they are about 10 weeks old. Then the young opossums ride around on their mother's back.

An opossum's tail is long and strong. The opossum uses it to hang from trees and prop itself up when it sits and eats roots, insects, fruit, and small animals. It can even carry things with its tail!

An opossum has an interesting way of defending itself. When an animal attacks, the opossum "plays dead" by lying very still. Soon the attacker walks away—and the opossum gets up and goes on its way.

LEACH SCHOOL LIBRARY

13

RED FOX

Few animals are as clever as the fox. When a fox is being hunted, it will run through a flock of sheep or wade through a stream. It knows this will make its scent hard to follow.

Foxes sometimes have the same mate all their lives. But they only live together when they are raising a family. 4-7 *pups* or *kits* are born in the spring. Their parents teach them how to hunt mice, squirrels, insects, and other things. When the fall comes, the kits go out on their own.

A fox's bushy tail is called a *brush.* When it sleeps, the fox wraps its brush around its body and face. This helps it keep warm.

TIMBER WOLF

Wolves live in large groups called *packs*. The pack is one big family. Brothers, sisters, cousins, and parents all live together. The pack will often howl in loud voices. This may sound spooky, but it is just the way wolves talk to each other.

The pack's leader is called the *alpha wolf*. His mate is the *alpha female*. In the spring, she gives birth to about 6 *cubs*. The whole pack takes care of the cubs and teaches them how to hunt large animals such as moose, deer, and elk.

PORCUPINE

Most of the time, a porcupine chews the bark off of trees. It is quiet and doesn't bother anyone. But if a porcupine is attacked, it has a very interesting way of defending itself. Its thick fur is covered with strong, sharp quills. These quills are very lightly attached to the porcupine's skin and have tiny hooks, called *barbs*, on the ends. If an attacker is hit by the porcupine's tail or touches the porcupine's body—ouch! The quills stick in the attacker's skin.

In the spring, a mother porcupine moves into a hollow log or a pile of branches and leaves. There she has a baby. The baby is born with all its quills.

BROWN BEAR

A mother bear takes good care of her *cubs.* 1-4 cubs are born in the winter, while the mother is sleeping in a warm cave or hollow log. The cubs stay with their mother for a year or two. Then they go out on their own.

Bears can't see or hear well, but they have a very good sense of smell. This helps them find roots, berries, and small animals to eat. Bears also catch fish in their big, strong paws. And they love honey so much they will take apart a beehive to get some. The bear's long, thick fur protects it from the angry bees.

BEAVER

If you have ever seen a dam made of mud and sticks in a stream, then you've seen the work of a beaver. Beavers cut down small trees with their sharp teeth. Then they trim these trees into logs and branches. The logs are stuck together with mud. Beavers also use logs and mud to make a snug, warm home called a *lodge.* The entrance to the lodge is deep underwater, so no enemies can get in.

Beavers have flat tails. They look like paddles. The beaver uses its tail to steer when it swims. And if danger is near, the beaver slaps its tail on the water. The loud *whack* tells other beavers to hurry to safety.

SKUNK

A skunk has a very good way of defending itself. First, it stamps its feet and hisses or growls. If the skunk's attacker doesn't run away, the skunk sprays it with a foul-smelling liquid. This liquid is called *musk*. It is made by a pair of glands near the base of the skunk's tail.

Skunks live underground or in hollow logs. They line their dens with leaves and grass. They sleep most of the day, but come out at night to hunt for food. A skunk will dig for insects and worms. It also likes to eat nuts, fruit, birds' eggs, mice, and other small animals.